CW01664398

TO

JESSICA

LOVE FROM

....

Jessica loves being under the sea. Whether it's exploring a sunken pirate ship, swimming with mighty whales or looking at big shells, she couldn't be happier.

But today was different. Jessica was about to meet the most majestic creature of the underwater world....

Jessica was gliding through the cool, clear water, hypnotised by the coral, when she heard something strange.

"Is that ... crying?" she said.

SOB! SOB! SOB!

Jessica swam towards the sound and stopped when she spotted an entrance to a deep, dark cave....

"I wonder what's in there?" Jessica thought as she drifted closer.

As she bobbed up and down a sea creature peeked out from the darkness!

"Err, he- hello?" he whispered.

Jessica could just about make out that he was pink with blue sticky-up hair. But he wasn't scary, he just looked very sad.

And he was carrying a gold crown.

The sea creature wasn't just any old sea creature – he was a king. But he might not be for much longer.

"I was having my afternoon snooze, and when I woke up the jewels from my crown were gone," he sniffled. "If I don't get them back, how can I be king?"

"Don't worry," said Jessica. "I'll help you find them. Whoever took them can't have gone far. Let's go!"

And so the search for the lost jewels began....

"There's one!" pointed Jessica.

"Oh no, the grumpy crabs have got it!" gasped the king.

SNAP! GRUMBLE, GRUMBLE! SNAP! SNAP!

Jessica quickly dodged round one, darted past another, ducked under a third and rescued the jewel from a snapping claw.

"I've got it!" she yelled.

"Quick, let's skedaddle," said the king. "They'll be grumpier than ever now!"

Up ahead, Jessica and the king saw a giant clamshell perched on a rock. Could a jewel be trapped inside?

"Hmm," said Jessica, "how do you get a clamshell to open up?"

"I don't know," said the king, "how do you get a clamshell to open up?"

"It's not a joke!" said Jessica, "but that gives me an idea...."

She grabbed a handful of seaweed and began to tickle.

HA HA HA! HA HA HA! HA HA HA!

The clamshell burst open and the king plucked out the jewel.

"Ta-dah, only two more left to find!" he cheered.

Suddenly, a dolphin whooshed past and darted upwards.

"Something fishy's going on," giggled Jessica, "let's go!"

They burst onto the surface where a pod of dolphins was jumping and spinning and diving.

SPLASH! SPLISH! SPLOSH!

And they were throwing around another jewel.

Jessica had to act fast. She threw her purse up in the air to trick the dolphins. Then, she quickly caught the jewel.

"Three down, only one to go!" she smiled.

The only place left on the reef they hadn't searched was ...

THE SEAWEED FOREST!

"Are you s-s-sure you want to g-g-go in there?" stuttered the king nervously.

Jessica looked up at the towering hairy branches swaying back and forth. Big, spooky eyes blinked back at her from the darkness, but that didn't stop her.

"I'll be fine!" said Jessica as she flicked on her torch.

Jessica hadn't been in an underwater forest before, but it was fun.

As she swam upwards she suddenly came face-to-face with the cutest thing she'd ever seen – a gigantic octopus.

The octopus looked startled and darted off. And as he did, eagle-eyed Jessica spotted the last jewel.

"Come back!" she shouted.

But the octopus disappeared.

Jessica needed a plan.

She kicked her flippers harder and harder and swam faster and faster through the seaweed to get ahead of the octopus.

Then she stopped, hid and kept very still.

It wasn't long before the seaweed started to rustle. She waited for just the right moment, and then....

"BOOOO!" yelled Jessica.

"AHHHHHHHH!" wailed the octopus.

Jessica quickly jumped out and rescued the final jewel.

Jessica carefully pressed the jewels into the king's crown and swam up to place it on his head.

"Ready?" asked Jessica.

"Ready!" smiled the king.

As Jessica lowered the crown all the fishy friends let out a big cheer, and all around them looked like awesome fireworks.

WOO-HOO! HOORAY!

"Jessica, you're my hero!" declared the king.

"I can't thank you enough," said the king. "If there's anything I can do for you, just name it."

"Well, there is one small thing," smiled Jessica. "Can you please let the jewel thieves out? They were only playing."

"Consider it done," said the king, "I guess they've learned their lesson now."

And with that, Jessica turned, waved goodbye and began to swim home, daydreaming of her next BIG adventure....

TIME OUT

MEET SANTA?
Maybe I'll...

Jessica, look out for more **Mini Adventures** books.
Go to www.orangutanbooks.co.uk

Story by Jane Kent
Illustrated by Jo Lindley
Designed by Jane Gollner

orangutan

First published by Orangutan Books in 2019
Hometown World Ltd, 1 Queen Street, Bath BA1 1HE

Visit
www.orangutanbooks.co.uk
Follow us @orangutanbooks

Copyright © Hometown World Ltd 2019
ISBN 978-1-78979-477-9
All rights reserved
Printed in Italy
HTW_PO201907

FSC www.fsc.org
MIX
Paper from responsible sources
FSC® C023419